Exits
and
Entrances

—

Athol Fugard

THEATRE COMMUNICATIONS GROUP
NEW YORK
2008

Exits and Entrances is published by Theatre Communications Group, Inc.,
520 Eighth Avenue, 24th Floor, New York, NY 10018-4156

This publication is made possible in part with public funds from the New York State Council on the Arts, a State Agency.

TCG books are exclusively distributed to the book trade by Consortium Book Sales and Distribution.

Library of Congress Cataloging-in-Publication Data
Fugard, Athol.
Exits and entrances / Athol Fugard.
p. cm.
ISBN-13: 978-1-55936-269-6
ISBN-10: 1-55936-269-3
1. Huguenet, André—Drama. 2. Actors—South Africa—Drama. I. Title.
PR9369.3.F8E95   2006
822'.914—dc22   2006013099

Cover design by Mark Melnick
Cover photo by Erich Lessing/Art Resource, NY
Text design and composition by Lisa Govan

First Edition, April 2008

To Gavyn,

From his oupa

$\mathcal{C}$ontents

Exits
and
Entrances

PRODUCTION HISTORY

Exits and Entrances received its world premiere in May 2004 at The Fountain Theatre in Los Angeles (Deborah Lawlor and Stephen Sachs, co-artistic directors; Simon Levy, producing director/dramaturg). Stephen Sachs directed the production; the set design was by David Potts, the lighting design was by Kathi O'Donohue, the sound design was by David B. Marling, the costume design was by Shon LeBlanc and the prop design was by Goar Galstyan; the production stage manager was Casey Decanay. The cast was:

THE PLAYWRIGHT	William Dennis Hurley
ANDRÉ HUGUENET	Morlan Higgins

The play received its South African premiere in July 2005 at the Baxter Theatre Centre in Cape Town. Janice Honeyman directed the production; the design was by Saul Radomsky and the lighting design was by Mannie Manim. The cast was:

THE PLAYWRIGHT	Jason Ralph
ANDRÉ HUGUENET	Sean Taylor

CHARACTERS

THE PLAYWRIGHT: twenty-nine years old in 1961; twenty-four in the flashback Labia Theatre scene. At twenty-four, he has all the conceits of youth and inexperience, but not offensively so.

ANDRÉ HUGUENET: fifty-five years old in 1961; fifty in the flashback Labia Theatre scene. A grand actor. Behind his imperious and commanding manner and sharp tongue is an insecure and lonely man.

SET

The main items are a table and chair that serve as the playwright's table in his Port Elizabeth apartment in 1961; a dressing-room table in the Labia Theatre, Cape Town, in 1956; and a dressing room table in the Port Elizabeth Opera House in 1961. There is also a costume rack with the various costumes that will be used in the play. At the director's discretion, there could also be a tired old armchair such as one finds in theatre dressing rooms the world over.

Author's Note

Thanks to Professor Marianne McDonald for her translation of *Oedipus the King*, made especially for use in this play.

1961. The Playwright, twenty-nine, at his table in Port Elizabeth. It is late at night and he is making an entry in his notebook. After a few minutes of writing, he puts down his pen and reads what he has written:

PLAYWRIGHT:

June 1961. My usual late-night walk around the park—full moon, the air heavy with dew and autumn fragrances—damp soil, moldy leaves and at one point a seductive whiff of jasmine. I was back in bed, lying awake in the dark, smoking a pipe, when church bells began to toll. It was midnight and I suddenly realized I was listening to the birth cries of the new Republic of South Africa. A few seconds after the bells, an engine whistle started up, down in the marshaling yards—some patriotic Afrikaner, no doubt, who kept it going for at least three minutes. By this time a few motorcar hooters had also joined in. All in all a celebration even more dreary than the few desultory noises that usher in the New Year here in the windy city. By 12:45 it was all over—the night left once again to the moon, the empty streets and sleeping houses, the crickets in the hedges and the dew falling drop by drop from the roof gutter.

This morning I caught a snatch of the inaugural ceremony on the radio—a DRC minister, in tones of deep and exaggerated reverence, thanking God for our young republic. When the commentator announced that the ceremony had "now reached the most solemn moment of all," I switched off. So there you have it—good-bye to the Union of South Africa and welcome to the young republic, out goes the queen and in comes our first Staats president. Arrivals and departures! And at a personal level as well: my dad off to hospital, where I think he will die; my three-week-old daughter newly arrived in my life from that same hospital; my new play out of my life and on its way to Johannesburg . . . and another small and unobtrusive exit—two inches at the bottom of an inside page of today's newspaper, reporting the death of "the great Afrikaans actor, André Huguenet" . . . found dead in his sister's home in Bloemfontein. No mention of the circumstances of his death, which doesn't really surprise me. I think I know what happened.

(From this point on he slips easily into a direct relationship with the audience.)

Impeccable timing, of course! Nothing would have made André happier than to stand up and walk out on that sanctimonious dominee thanking the Almighty and telling the volk that they were God's chosen people. His exit coincides so neatly with the birth of our Republiek I could almost believe he planned it that way. Because if there was one stage skill that André had truly mastered, it was timing—that instinct for the perfect moment, the precise second for the word, the action, the gesture, or in an instance that I will never, never forget: the cry. It was that moment in *Oedipus the King* when the old Shepherd puts the last piece of the puzzle into place, and as a result, Oedipus knows that he has murdered his father and slept with his mother, that his children are also his brothers and sisters. The Shepherd's last line to him is: "If you, Master, are that man, then you are indeed the most miserable of all men."

André, as Oedipus, standing at the top of the steps in front of the doors of his Theban palace, became very still, and we ordinary mortals held our breaths and waited. In those terribly silent seconds it seemed as if the whole world was waiting, and at the point when you thought you could no longer endure it and would have to scream, at that precise moment, not a second too soon or too late, André opened his mouth and out of it came the most awful cry that any member of that audience had ever heard. It sounded as if he had somehow reached down deep into himself and was dragging his genitals up through his body and throat and hanging them out of his mouth for all of us to spit on and curse. And that was not just one memorable performance! Oh no. André knew it was *the* moment of the play, so he hit that mark with uncanny accuracy virtually every night. I know what I am talking about because I was there onstage with him. Five years ago, the Labia Theatre in Cape Town. In those days the pool of local acting talent was very shallow so poor André had ended up having to cast me as that old Shepherd who clung so desperately to his ankles every night imploring him to stop his questions. I was twenty-four years old and my only stage experience had been in a couple of amateur productions.

(The Playwright wheels the costume rack onstage. On the table he lays out a stage-makeup kit, then prepares a mug of hot water, lemon and honey.)

I shared his dressing room because I also doubled as his dogsbody, fetching and carrying and serving him in whatever way I could. That production of *Oedipus the King* celebrated his thirtieth year on the stage. He was then fifty years old.

(The scene segues into 1956, the Labia Theatre dressing room. Offstage André is heard cursing in Afrikaans: "Hou jou fockin bek! Luis gat!"

A harassed and irritable André makes an entrance and sits down at the table where the Playwright has laid out André's makeup kit, etc.)

ANDRÉ *(As he starts his preparations for the performance)*: Young men with ugly knees should not wear short trousers . . .
PLAYWRIGHT: Who are you talking about?
ANDRÉ: You mean you didn't notice?
PLAYWRIGHT: Billy?
ANDRÉ: Who else. And did you see the tackies he was wearing—Oh my God!—looked as if he had two of those poisonous Karoo locusts for feet. Enough, Zeus! Enough! Mind you, a sight like that would be as good a reason for Oedipus blinding himself as discovering who he's

been in bed with all this time. So . . . *(Heavy sigh)* . . . here
we go again.

PLAYWRIGHT: Are you nervous?

ANDRÉ *(Disdainfully)*: Good God no. If this was a London
opening, then yes there might have been a little flutter,
an added charge of adrenaline over and above the one
I always get from performance. But in front of those half-
aan-die-slaap domkoppe we are going to have out there
tonight with their little notebooks and pencils, the mother
city's little coterie of theatre intellectuals? No, sweet-
heart. Most emphatically no. I have bred antibodies to
the bite of those little vipers. *(Suddenly suspicious and insecure)* But why do you ask? Do you think I should be?

PLAYWRIGHT: No. You're magnificent, and they'd have to be
very fast asleep in their seats not to see that. But you did
get some of your words wrong again in the run-through
this afternoon.

ANDRÉ *(Testily)*: Only because I knew my skirt was too short
and that the front row would be looking up it and seeing
my jockstrap. But of course that stupid cow wouldn't listen to me when I warned her about that. Designer my arse!
So where did I go wrong?

PLAYWRIGHT: The opening scene and then a couple of bad
ones with Jocasta.

ANDRÉ: Get your script—the first scene—give me my cues.

(They read the opening scene of Oedipus the King *while André
settles down at his table and applies his makeup for the role.)*

"Citizens of this city that Cadmus founded, why are you
here? . . ."

PLAYWRIGHT *(Correcting him)*: ". . . why have you come
here . . ."

ANDRÉ: Come now my little poephol, really . . .

PLAYWRIGHT: That is what Sophocles wrote.

ANDRÉ *(Trying again)*: "Citizens of this city that Cadmus founded, why have you come here? What is it that you want from me? Why do I smell incense and hear prayers and hymns . . ."

PLAYWRIGHT: " . . . hymns and prayers . . ."

ANDRÉ: " . . . hear hymns and prayers and the cries of people weeping?"

PLAYWRIGHT: Once again.

ANDRÉ: Stop bullying me.

PLAYWRIGHT: Do you want to get it right?

ANDRÉ *(Starting again)*: "Citizens of this city that Cadmus founded, why have you come here? What is it that you want from me?

I see you wear wreaths and carry sacred branches. I smell incense and hear hymns and prayers, and the cries of people weeping. Your suffering is obvious, so I, Oedipus, known to you all as your king, have come myself to find out what I can do.

Old man, I see you are the leader of these people.

Speak to me. If you have something to ask of me, do not be afraid to tell me what you want. I'll do what I can. I am not without pity."

PLAYWRIGHT: " . . . I am not a man without pity . . ."

ANDRÉ *(Sudden suspicion)*: Your concern for the printed word makes me suspect the worst.

PLAYWRIGHT: Which is? . . .

ANDRÉ: That you have literary ambitions?

PLAYWRIGHT: Yes. You guessed right. I want to be a playwright.

ANDRÉ: Lord have mercy on us. Another one.

PLAYWRIGHT: I'm dead serious, André.

ANDRÉ: Lord have mercy on us! Another one.

PLAYWRIGHT: I'm dead serious, André.

ANDRÉ: Which is cause for even greater concern. Can I be so impertinent as to ask what makes you think you can write a play? . . . Or is that something that just anybody can do?

PLAYWRIGHT: My wife. She pointed out that straight dialogue makes up more than half of the short stories I've written, so why not have a go at a play.

ANDRÉ: Oh I like that! Like the good old Sophocles: "Let's have a go at a play."

PLAYWRIGHT: You're still laughing at me.

ANDRÉ: Oh no, dear boy. What you heard there was despair, not mirth. But enough. Let's get on with it.

PLAYWRIGHT *(Prompting from the script):* "I pity you. I see that you are sick . . ."

(André paces around the dressing room as he runs his lines, giving us glimpses of his performance as Oedipus.)

ANDRÉ: "I pity you. I see that you are sick, but no one is as sick as I am. Each of you are sick individually, but I am sick because I grieve for the whole city, for you and for myself. You have not awakened me from some numb sleep without thought and tears for you; in my mind I have been wandering down many paths, searching for . . . searching for . . ." *(Impatiently)* Wake up, boy! What am I searching for?

PLAYWRIGHT: Different solutions.

ANDRÉ: ". . . down many paths searching for different solutions. This I think best: I sent Creon, my wife's brother, to Delphi, to Phoebus Apollo, to find out what I can say or do to save the city. It's been such long time since he left that I'm worried about him, but when he returns, I would be a worthless man if I didn't follow the god's advice."

PLAYWRIGHT *(Sincere admiration):* You're wonderful.

ANDRÉ *(Stopped short—genuinely affected):* Really?

PLAYWRIGHT: Oh yes. Looks like nothing on paper but when you speak them . . . I don't know . . . I get goose pimples watching you when I stand there in the wings. It's like you become him. How do you do it?

ANDRÉ *(Studying his face in his dressing-table mirror)*: We have a lot in common. He must have been about my age as he stood there in front of his palace. Even though I didn't murder my father and sleep with my mother, the gods appear to have also singled me out for special attention. A bit of boereseun hubris, not so? Likening myself to Oedipus the King! Like him I also started off trying to run away from myself. Maybe I still am. Vervloekte André! That is what I should have called my autobiography.

PLAYWRIGHT *(Laughing)*: Vervloekte?

ANDRÉ: Cursed.

PLAYWRIGHT: It's a damned good title for a short story: "Vervloekte André"!

ANDRÉ *(Outraged)*: Short story! My life? What are you talking about? My childhood alone is a volume on its own. I'm not joking! To be who and what I am in this god-forsaken country feels very much like a curse at times, my dear boy.

PLAYWRIGHT: So how did it all start?

ANDRÉ: What?

PLAYWRIGHT: Your theatre career?

ANDRÉ: Read my book.

PLAYWRIGHT: What's it called?

ANDRÉ: *Applous: Die Kronieke van 'n Toneelspeler.*

PLAYWRIGHT: Oh—it's in Afrikaans.

ANDRÉ *(Heavy sarcasm)*: Yes, and I do apologize for that to all you very superior English-speaking South Africans!

PLAYWRIGHT: Come now, André, it's just that Afrikaans was never one of my good subjects at school.

ANDRÉ: Of course! But why bother about that, because nothing of any significance has ever been written in that language. Not so?

PLAYWRIGHT: For your information, André, my mother is an Afrikaner.

ANDRÉ: Shh! Don't say that so loudly. Someone might hear, darling, and what then!

PLAYWRIGHT *(Laughing)*: You're terrible.

So it was a school play?

ANDRÉ *(His turn for a laugh)*: School play? No, my dear boy. School plays were not on the curriculum of the Dopper School in Zastron Street in 1916, with its motto: Eerlikheid en Christelikheid. And even if they had been, my Dopper family would have done everything in their power to keep me out of something as threatening to my virtue and salvation as that. I mean, don't you know how wicked and sinful all actors and actresses are? Haven't you heard about the terrible goings-on in the theatre? The drunkenness? The sexual orgies? *(Sighs)* If only it were true! How much more fun this would all be!

But no. Not at school. If you really want to know, it all started in the Bloemfontein Town Hall. That is where, at the tender age of eleven, that innocent Gerhardus Petrus Borstlap was seduced and corrupted beyond all possibility of redemption.

PLAYWRIGHT *(Laughing)*: Who? . . .

ANDRÉ: Gerhardus Petrus Borstlap. That is my real name— and if you tell anybody, old Shepherd, you will die onstage tonight when I get my hands on you.

Yes, the Bloemfontein Town Hall. A most unlikely setting for a seduction, but that is where it happened. You want to know who the dastardly villain was that robbed me of my innocence? A swan. A dying swan. *(Settling in with relish to the telling of his story)* One night, pretending that he was going to an extra organ lesson, "the Little Predikant" (my nickname in the family)—I was being groomed, you see, to be a dominee in the Dopper church—the Little Predikant took all his pocket money and the pennies he had saved up (he needed five shillings), queued up with a lot of other opregte Afrikaners and bought a ticket to see a vision of grace and beauty that will stay with him to his dying day.

(Pause.)

Pavlova.

PLAYWRIGHT: The Russian ballerina! In Bloemfontein? . . .

ANDRÉ: In 1916.

I didn't even know she existed until they put up a big poster outside the town hall: PAVLOVA. THE GREAT RUSSIAN BALLERINA IN "THE DYING SWAN." So I asked my mother about her, and did she then give me a lecture! You must know we Bloemfontein Borstlaps were a strict Dopper family. Eternal damnation! Nothing less. Straight to hell if I went anywhere near that wicked woman and her shameless dance! The devil had sent her because of all the sinning that was going on in Bloemfontein, which of course meant that I just had to see her for myself. But it wasn't easy! Sitting there in the hall waiting for the "konsert" to start I had a lot of time trying to imagine what hell was going to be like. The only reason I stayed there in my seat and didn't run back home was because I could see I would have a lot of other good Doppers for company on my way down to the big braaivleis. But then the music started, the lights in the hall went down, the curtain went up . . . *(Pause)* . . . and she floated onto the stage.

It was a moment that changed my life. You must understand, dear boy, the world I was growing up in was ugly—just plain no-frills ugly. It was a railway camp. My father worked for the railways, you see, so all of us—my father and my mother and my oupa, and me and my sister and my brother—were squashed into one of those ugly little houses, squashed in among all the other ugly little houses. And they all looked the same. If it wasn't for the numbers you wouldn't know which one was yours. No place to escape. Nowhere to hide from the big bully boys in the camp who were always after the little "Dopper Moffie"—that was my other nickname—because he didn't play rugby with them.

That is what Pavlova did to me that night in the Bloemfontein Town Hall. She opened my eyes to a different world. When she floated out into the blue light on the stage I knew that I was looking at a world where I would be safe, where I would be able to escape being "Vervloekte Gerhardus Petrus Borstlap," the "Dopper Moffie," and dream that I was somebody else. *(Shakes his head, laughing wryly)*

PLAYWRIGHT: And so you did!

ANDRÉ: Did I really? Did Oedipus escape the fate he was running from?

Anyway, what I didn't know then—and maybe just as well, because if I had I most certainly wouldn't be here with you now—was how much snot en trane and angst you have to live through before you can really start dreaming up there, and even then how infrequently that happens.

PLAYWRIGHT: Do you think Pavlova was dreaming up there that night in Bloemfontein?

ANDRÉ: I doubt it. Most probably counting the number of people in the audience and working out the take for the night. But I am sure there were times when she had her dreams. You see, there has to be a dream. Somewhere along the line she had to believe she was the most beautiful, the most graceful of all the creatures in the world, and to believe that with every fiber of her being and, having dreamt that, she also had to feel the first touch of death and try, hopelessly, to escape it, discover that her magnificent wings could no longer lift her off the

ground, feel that touch turn into a cruel, unrelenting
hold on her whole life . . .

PLAYWRIGHT *(Totally under André's spell)*: Wow! That must
have been something.
Dreams! I never thought of it like that. Maybe that's
what I'm doing when I write, what all creativity is
about. The hard labor of dreams!
So for you, there was also a moment when you
believed you were Oedipus standing in front of your
palace in Thebes?

ANDRÉ: Oh yes. Weird isn't it. I briefly escape my curse by
pretending to be a man who can't escape his. That is
what our play is all about you know. In thinking he was
running away from his fate, Oedipus runs right into its
arms and its terrible embrace.

PLAYWRIGHT: Are you going to dream tonight?

ANDRÉ: No, not tonight. Those little vipers with their pencils and notebooks take the magic out of everything.
The awful truth about our business is that the audience
has to give you permission to dream. But stop now.
You're making me nervous. What's next?

PLAYWRIGHT: The scene with Jocasta. At the rehearsal this
afternoon you—

ANDRÉ: I know. I know. What do you expect? I'm carrying the
whole show you know. Working with amateurs! I know
you try your best, dear boy, but dear God, it does make
me suffer you know. Anyway if it makes you feel better
I can tell you that you are most certainly not the worst.
So what's my cue?

PLAYWRIGHT: It's Jocasta's line . . . "I think I should know
what it is that bothers you."

*(The scene with Jocasta. André, now in costume, deepens his
commitment to the role, though there are still stumbles in his
lines, which the Playwright corrects.)*

ANDRÉ: "I won't deny you this, now that forebodings haunt
me. Who more than you should hear about all that has
happened to me?

My father was Polybus, King of Corinth, and my
mother Merope, a Dorian. In everything I was privi-
leged above all others in the kingdom.

Then something happened, which was indeed
offensive, but hardly something that should have upset
me as much as it did. A man, whom too much wine had
made loose-tongued, said that I wasn't my father's child.
I was deeply disturbed and bridled at the insult. The next
day I went to my father and mother and they were furi-
ous at the drunken lout.

Although their reaction in some measure placated
me, grim doubts continued to torment me.

Without disclosing my intention, I went to Delphi
to consult the Pythian oracle, but Apollo ignored what
I'd asked, and instead told me other horrible things:
I would have sexual intercourse with my mother and
sire a brood that other men would shudder to see. In
addition to this, I would be the killer of my father.

After this, guided by the stars, I left my home,
Corinth, meaning never to see it again, so that those
dreadful prophecies would never be fulfilled.

I walked to the place where you say the king died.
I'll tell you the truth. When I came to the crossroads,
I met a man, riding in a carriage, with a herald, just as
you said. The driver and the old man tried to force me
off the road. In my fury I struck out at the driver, who
was trying to push me away. When he saw this, the old
man waited until I was coming past and then hit me full
on the head with his double-pronged stick, which he
used to goad the horses.

I gave back double what he delivered: I struck him
full on with my staff and knocked him out of the car-

riage. By then I was beside myself with rage. I killed him and then I killed them all.

But if it turns out that this stranger was indeed Laius, then I would be the most miserable of all men: no one more hated by the gods. No stranger, no citizen could invite me into his home, and no one speak to me: everyone must drive me away. Only I am to blame for this curse that I laid on myself.

I have touched you in the bed of the dead man with the same hands that murdered him. Am I a criminal? Am I an unholy monster? Must I run away and not see my family? May I not return to my native soil, because then I risk marrying my mother and killing my father Polybus, who raised me and gave me life? Wouldn't someone be right to say that this fate comes from a savage god? O God, O God, by all that is holy, let me die now rather than live to see such a day! Banish me away from the sight of men before I commit such filthy crimes."

PLAYWRIGHT: This is where the play starts to get scary.

You know what little Jennifer—your Antigone— said to me this afternoon? "Why doesn't he stop and listen to the prophet and his wife? That way we could have a happy ending tonight."

ANDRÉ *(An exultant, almost brutal laugh):* "Stop and listen"? He can't! He is Oedipus!

PLAYWRIGHT: And so are you.

ANDRÉ: What do you mean?

PLAYWRIGHT: Just what you said earlier. You are like him in so many ways.

ANDRÉ: Those being . . . my temper?

PLAYWRIGHT: That's one for sure. We're all terrified of you.

ANDRÉ: But what else?

(The young Playwright is reluctant to say more.)

Come on! Speak up, boy.

PLAYWRIGHT: There! The way you said that.

ANDRÉ: I see. Arrogance.

PLAYWRIGHT: You could call it that.

ANDRÉ: And is that all you could charge me and Oedipus with? What about pride? He is after all a king talking to his subjects and I am a professional actor in a company of amateurs. Vanity? Jocasta fell in love with him and my audiences will with me. Selfishness? Once he started out he didn't give a damn about anybody else and neither do I when I am up there on the stage.

And that, dear boy, is why it is so glorious to be up there as him, making all those terrible fatal mistakes and knowing that for once it isn't me.

PLAYWRIGHT: And what about the end?

ANDRÉ: Of what? The play?

PLAYWRIGHT: Yes.

ANDRÉ: Why? Haven't you seen it? He walks off as blind as the prophet who tried to warn him.

PLAYWRIGHT: But do you feel sorry for him?

ANDRÉ: Good heavens no! Pity him? Of what use would that be? His fate is sealed . . . and by himself what's more. It's there on the last page of the script and nothing can change it! Up there tonight my actor's soul will lust for those final moments of his unspeakable agony and terrible torment. I've come to love the taste of that stage blood dripping from my face . . .

(. . . André is now fully dressed as Oedipus, and after he applies the stage blood, he rises from the table. He leaves the reality of the dressing room and gives his full-blooded stage performance of the blind king at the end of Sophocles' play, with the Playwright throwing him his cues from the darkness at the back.)

Aiai aiai, such pain!
Where can I go?

What breeze carries my voice, and where?
Where has fate brought me?

The pain of it! Pain again.
The memory of what I have done
Lays into me like a lash on open wounds.

Apollo did it, Apollo, friends:
He caused all this evil and made me suffer.
But it was me—
My hand alone struck out my eyes.
Why should I see?
I am a man for whom sight holds nothing sweet.

What is left for me to see, or love,
Or what words could be pleasant to hear?
Throw me out, throw me away,
One who stinks of death,
A man most hated and most cursed by the gods.

Damned be that shepherd
Who released my feet from their cruel ties,
Snatched me from death, and saved me.
He did me no favor.
If I had died, there would have been no suffering
For those close, nor for myself.

I would not have killed my father,
Nor be known as the husband of she who bore me.
Now I am a godless man, child of cursed parents,
A man who conceived children as siblings
To those his own father had conceived.

If there is an evil that surpasses evil itself,
Oedipus claims it.

Three roads, and a hidden valley,
A small cluster of trees,
And that narrow path where three roads meet:
You drank my blood, and the blood of my father
That I myself shed.

Marriage, marriage, you made me
And you made more from the same seed:
You brought to light fathers who were brothers,
Children of incest,
Brides who were both wives and
Mothers to their husbands—
Yes, you engendered
The most shameful acts that man can do.

But it is not right to speak
Of what was not right to do;
So for the sake of the gods, hide me away,
As soon as possible, out of sight,
Or kill me: throw me into the ocean
Where you will never see me again.
Show yourselves to be good men, and
Be kind enough to touch this suffering man.
Do it, and don't be afraid.
I alone am polluted:
I am the only man who must bear this suffering.

*(Segue back to the dressing room table. André, tasting the stage
blood on one of his fingers, behaves like someone in a state of
shock. The Playwright steps forward and helps him take off his
costume and makeup. While he is doing this he talks directly
to the audience:)*

PLAYWRIGHT: That opening night was, on the face of it, a great success. A full house gave us a standing ovation at the end, and the critics were all very respectful of the occasion and wrote glowingly about André's performance. In spite of all that, however, we were soon playing to very small audiences and in the last week there were a couple of nights when we thought that André might even cancel the show because so few people had turned up. The atmosphere backstage became depressingly muted, and André, even more moody than usual. What I didn't know at the time was that he had borrowed heavily to finance his "celebratory production" and that at the end of it he would be bankrupt. But as I realized when I eventually read his autobiography some years later, André was no stranger to that state of affairs. His thirty years of single-minded and unwavering dedication to Afrikaans theatre has not been richly rewarded. The sound that came to me most often from the pages of his *Chronicles of an Actor* was an echo of the few seconds of thin and embarrassed applause that we bowed to every night in the last week of the run. On a couple of occasions it had already died away into silence when André stepped forward to take a last individual bow. But he took it nevertheless and with defiant aplomb, as if a full house was out there and on its feet shouting, "Bravo!"

(He now speaks directly to André:)

Yes. "Bravo, André." That is what that miserable audience should have been shouting. You can go home tonight feeling very satisfied. In my opinion they got the best show of the entire run! God you were good!
I think that was my best one as well.

(André says nothing.)

I'm getting on your nerves aren't I.

ANDRÉ: Yes you are.

PLAYWRIGHT: Sorry. I'll shut up.

(A few seconds of silence.)

ANDRÉ: "Home." What does that word mean to you?

PLAYWRIGHT: "Home"? I suppose the place where you live . . . you know, where your family is . . . where you go to at the end of a day's work. I've never really thought about it much. It's always just been there. My mom's home in Port Elizabeth when I was growing up. And I suppose now it's the Sea Point flat where I live with my wife. *(Intrigued by the question)* Why do you ask?

ANDRÉ: You used the word so easily.

PLAYWRIGHT: Did I?

ANDRÉ: Yes. You said I could go "home tonight very . . . satisfied . . ." or something to that effect.

PLAYWRIGHT: And so you should. What's wrong with that?

ANDRÉ *(Shaking his head)*: I won't be "going home," I'll be leaving it.

PLAYWRIGHT: I don't understand.

ANDRÉ: Thirty years ago, like you, I also used the word very easily one night in a conversation . . . you know, unthinkingly . . . assuming, like you, that its meaning was very simple. I was talking to Eugène Marais. You know who he is?

PLAYWRIGHT: No.

ANDRÉ: You English!

PLAYWRIGHT: I'm not. I'm a South African.

ANDRÉ: Not until you find out who Eugène Marais is and have read him!

(Pause.)

It was in the office of *Die Vaderland*—a Pretoria newspaper. We were both on the staff—I couldn't find work as an actor so I was filling in time as a reporter of "social and cultural events." It was late at night and I had gone back to the office to write a review about a very bad performance I had just seen. *(A little laugh)* Poor Anna Klaasen! I was a real bitch. I can still remember the opening line of my review: "A fading star of the Netherlands' theatrical universe wandered into our remote little galaxy last night." Marais was also in the office—fast asleep at his desk. "Oom Eugène"! That is what we all—very respectfully!—called him. He woke up and we eventually got talking. Before that night, like everyone else, I had politely kept my distance from the great writer, but there in the office, just the two of us, I was able to break through the barrier of my awe and respect and really talk to him. When he heard that I was really an actor, he was interested and encouraged me to tell him about myself. I did. I told him about my vision of the Afrikaans theatre of the future!

PLAYWRIGHT: You had a vision?

ANDRÉ: Yes. The height of madness wasn't it. A young man with a vision in this country! Believe it or not but vervloekte André thought that theatre could liberate our people—break the shackles that the verkrampte dominees and politicians were forging around our minds and souls. Anyway . . . I also shared with Oom Eugène the secret of my real name and told him that "home" was a strict Dopper family in Bloemfontein. Out of politeness I asked him where his "home" was. He smiled and then held up the sheet of blank paper that was on his desk in front of him. I didn't know what the gesture meant but I was too shy to reveal my ignorance by asking, so I just nodded as if I understood and we went on to talk about other things. Afterwards I thought a lot about that moment and I did finally get his meaning. He was a writer. A great writer. Words on paper is what his life had been all about. That blank sheet of paper was his real home. I am an actor. A good actor. For thirty years I've been up there "on the boards" acting. The stage is my real home. When I am up there, as cursed and reckless Oedipus, or neurotic Hamlet, or lovesick Hassan or any of the other emotional cripples I've played in my time, I know who I am, what I am, and why I am what I am. What a divine irony! My greatest security, my most certain sense of myself lies in pretending to be someone else. So what did you say—"go home satisfied"? No. What you thought was my home, little snotneus, is a bleak hotel room with a couple of well-traveled and half-unpacked suitcases. There've been hundreds like it and God alone knows how many lie ahead of me. Do you understand now?

PLAYWRIGHT: Yes I do. I'm sorry.

ANDRÉ *(Sharply)*: For what? For who? Me? I am not asking for your pity! My home gives me as much and maybe more than yours will ever give you. You have a pretty wife waiting for you? I had a queen tonight. I've had an Ophelia swooning for me. I've had as much love poured over me in my home as you will ever have in yours. And what is more I was given a golden tongue to sing mine out loud! *(Laughs joyously)*

(The last of the makeup is off. The towel wrapped around his head suggests a turban as he recites lines from James Elroy Flecker's play Hassan:)

How splendid in the morning glows the lily;
with what grace he throws

His supplication to the rose:
do roses nod the head, Yasmin?
... Shower down thy love, O burning bright!
for one night or the other night
Will come the Gardener in white,
and gathered flowers are dead, Yasmin!

O stay, Yasmin, you are too beautiful and I too bold. I am nothing, and you are the Queen of the Stars of Night. But the thought of you is twisted in the strings of my heart; I burn with love of you, Yasmin. Put me to the proof, my lady; there is nothing I could not do for your bright eyes. I would cross the salt desert and wrest the cup of the water of life from the Jinn that guards it; I would walk to the barriers of the world and steal the roc's egg from its diamond nest. I would swim the seven oceans, and cross the five islands to rob Solomon ben Dawud of his ring in the palace where he lies sleeping in the silence and majesty of uncorrupting death. And I would slip the ring on your finger and make you mistress of the spirits of the air—but would you love me? Could you love me, do you love me, Yasmin?

So don't feel sorry for me, dear boy. Because if you think I envy that emotional bog that the happily married normal people of this world flounder around in and call home, you are sorely mistaken. If pity is in order, then it is rather I who must feel that for you. Your "sacred vows," little darling, have shackled you for life. I never worry about adultery in my home. I am bonded by my love of the fair lady I woo onstage for only the duration of the play.

PLAYWRIGHT *(Laughing and applauding)*: Wow that was good!

ANDRÉ: Thank you.

PLAYWRIGHT: But who was Yasmin? Where does she come from?

ANDRÉ: *Hassan* by James Elroy Flecker! London, 1950. And on that occasion the stage of the Cambridge Theatre was my home.

PLAYWRIGHT: And now? Quo vadis, Domine?

ANDRÉ: Stop showing off and speak English.

PLAYWRIGHT: What's next?

ANDRÉ *(Airily)*: They're talking to me about Lear.

PLAYWRIGHT: Think you'll do it?

ANDRÉ: Maybe. Maybe it's time now to settle down to a quiet family life. Just think of it. Three lovely daughters. That should be fun, don't you think? Daddy and his darlings!

(The Playwright leaves André and comes downstage to talk directly to the audience.)

PLAYWRIGHT: Our paths crossed again for the second and last time in 1961. Only five years had passed since that production of *Oedipus* in Cape Town but it might well have been fifty because of all that had happened during that time to him, to me, and to our country. Our meeting took place in his dressing room in the Opera House in Port Elizabeth—it was just a few days after the first anniversary of Sharpeville. I had just returned from London. I was still trying to write plays and I had gone over there with a couple of them under my arm, but without any success. Back in Port Elizabeth I was writing another one and waiting for the birth of my daughter. As for André . . .

(André leaves his table and, wearing only his underclothes, comes forward, goes down on his knees and scrubs the floor.)

I hadn't stayed in touch with him during those five years, so when I saw posters around town advertising: ANDRÉ HUGUENET IN *THE PRISONER* I wasted no time in buying a ticket. I sat down in the theatre with expectations colored by my still vivid memories of his arrogant and proud Oedipus. I was in for a surprise.

(The Playwright goes back to the costume rack while André delivers the following speech:)

ANDRÉ *(Scrubbing the floor)*:
> Three nines are twenty-seven, four nines are thirty-six, five nines are forty-five, six nines are fifty-four, seven nines are sixty-three, eight nines are seventy-two, four eights are thirty-two, six elevens are sixty-six . . .

(Pauses in his polishing and realizes his mind is wandering. He starts again:)

> Nines. Seven nines are sixty-three, eight nines are seventy-two, nine nines are eighty-one, ten nines are ninety. Once ten is ten, two tens are twenty, three tens are thirty. Four tens are forty, five tens are fifty, six tens are sixty, seven tens are seventy . . .

(Straightens up and kneels in prayer.)

> Consider and hear me, oh Lord, my God, lighten my eyes lest I sleep the sleep of death . . . lest mine enemy say: I have prevailed against him.

(Louder, shouting down his thoughts:)

Rejoice not against me, O mine enemy: when I fall I shall rise, when I sit in darkness the Lord shall be a light to me. Set a watch, O Lord, before my mouth, keep thou the door of my lips.

(The Playwright comes down from the costume rack with the costume of a Cardinal. He speaks as he helps André into it.)

PLAYWRIGHT: The setting is a prison and the prisoner is a Cardinal in the Catholic Church of a middle-European country. The totalitarian government of this country finds it necessary to destroy the Cardinal, whose independence of spirit is a danger to them. He resists all their efforts to break him and make him sign a false confession until they find his one weak spot—a deep sense of personal guilt.

ANDRÉ *(In performance, his hand outstretched as if to touch something in front of him)*:
My mother. My mother. How old she looks. Old and innocent. Requiem aeternam dona— I never learned to pray for her. I never could pray for her.
    Oh, that cant phrase. Heredity. What else is my flesh but her flesh, where else did I get this crawling body that I'm buried in? All right, environment! The environment of a bed in the other room, listening to new feet blundering up the staircase, the whispering and the smothered laughter, and the bedsprings screeching beyond the stupid flowered paper on the wall! Remembering the smell of the woman who bent over you to try and kiss you good night. Where, before I was born or after it, would I find a heart?

Chastity, temperance, fortitude—but no love. I can serve men, or God, or my country, but I can't care. Open it up, tear it open, look for a heart—there's nothing there!

Write that I am the son of my mother, and my whole life a fantasy to hide me. Write that I lied my way through school and stole my way to a scholarship. Write that I became a priest for my own glory and that all my service was to my own spiritual pride. Write that I never had any love—love of the heart—for God. I never had a heart. The only prayer I ever prayed was, "Lord, I believe—help Thou my unbelief."

As for the people—write that I posed and postured for them. I ate when they were hungry. Tell them that when they called me in the night my first thought was anger. A woman dying in childbirth, uselessly, of a dead child, a man on the railway siding hanging mangled and screaming in the jaws of a crane, and my first thought when they woke me to go to them was anger, hatred of their stupidity and their suffering. I prayed for forgiveness but I knew I had no heart.

Let them see me in the weakness of the flesh and the meanness of the spirit. That will be degradation, that will be shame enough to burn the past and come through the flames, free.

(Segue back to the dressing room. We see a changed André— he is quieter, the abrasive edges have all but gone.)

PLAYWRIGHT: Bravo! Bravo!
ANDRÉ: My dear boy! Thank you. Thank you.

(They embrace.)

You should have told me you were coming. I would have organized a couple of comps.

PLAYWRIGHT: I came alone.

ANDRÉ: Divorced already? Congratulations!

PLAYWRIGHT: No, still married, but my wife is on the point of giving birth to our first child.

ANDRÉ: Oh dear! So then my sympathies instead. You do know don't you that babies cry a hell of a lot and can be very smelly.

PLAYWRIGHT: I'm prepared.

(André starts to take off his costume.)

Can I help? I've had experience as a dresser you know.

ANDRÉ: I remember. You were in fact quite good—and since you volunteer . . . There's a kettle back there, dear boy, do you think you could do the usual?

PLAYWRIGHT: You bet . . . hot water, lemon juice and honey.

(André laughs.)

That was a wonderful performance, André.

ANDRÉ: Thank you.

PLAYWRIGHT: So . . . *(Searching for the word)*

ANDRÉ: What?

PLAYWRIGHT: Different.

ANDRÉ: In what way? Different from what?

PLAYWRIGHT: From what I had expected.

ANDRÉ: Which was?

PLAYWRIGHT: I didn't know this play—it's a damned good one incidentally—so all that magnificent arrogance and pride of your Oedipus was in my mind when I sat there waiting for the curtain to go up.

ANDRÉ: The Cardinal has his fair share of those qualities as well.

PLAYWRIGHT: Yes, but he ends up scrubbing the floor! Your Oedipus never did. Even with his eyes out, his wife and mother dead, he was somehow still Oedipus the King! That scene tonight when you were down on your knees was incredible, very moving.

ANDRÉ: There's no great art to scrubbing a floor you know. Just get down there and do it. Anyway, I've had a lot of practice at it lately.

PLAYWRIGHT: In what way?

ANDRÉ: Oh . . . just life . . . you know, the usual ups and downs.

PLAYWRIGHT: Humility! That's the word I'm looking for. What I saw tonight was a journey from arrogant pride to humility! If I had to write a review of tonight's performance, that would have been my opening line.

ANDRÉ: The mighty brought low.

PLAYWRIGHT: Yes—which—if you don't mind me saying it—your Oedipus never really was you know.

ANDRÉ *(Thoughtful)*: How interesting. *(Changing the subject)* But what about you? Still married, soon to be a father . . . what else?

PLAYWRIGHT: Still writing.

ANDRÉ: Still plays?

PLAYWRIGHT: Can't do anything else! —And waiting for the baby. I suppose I'm also waiting for my own father to die?

ANDRÉ: That sounds a bit oedipal, dear boy.

PLAYWRIGHT: We were in fact very close. When I was a young boy. We still call each other "chum." If I could give him a couple of the years that I've got left, I would do so very happily.

ANDRÉ: What is wrong with him?

PLAYWRIGHT: Everything. When he does pass on I suppose the death certificate will talk about the gangrene in what is left of his crippled leg as the likely cause of death. But I think the real truth about my chum is that he's dying of unimportance.

ANDRÉ: What do you mean?

PLAYWRIGHT: Nobody needs him anymore. None of us have any space for him in our lives. We're all too busy, too full of our own importance to realize . . . that he is still there.

ANDRÉ: Unimportance! Yes, indeed . . . a dangerous disease. It can easily kill a man. How did he catch it? From you?

PLAYWRIGHT: Maybe. I'm certainly one of the main carriers. I let a lot of things crowd him out of my life . . . you know, my wonderful career, et cetera, et cetera. And now it's too late to do anything about it. *(Embarrassed)* Listen to me! I'm sorry. I didn't come backstage to confess my sins of omission and commission to the Cardinal.

ANDRÉ: Don't apologize, dear boy. *(Changing the subject)* So tell me about your writing. Still plays.

PLAYWRIGHT: Yep! I took a couple of them over to London but nobody was interested.

ANDRÉ: But you persist.

PLAYWRIGHT: I've just about finished a new one. I think it stands a bit of a chance.

ANDRÉ: I'm nervous, but I have to ask: What's it about?

PLAYWRIGHT: Two brothers.

ANDRÉ: That's a good start.

PLAYWRIGHT: Coloreds.

ANDRÉ: Oh.

PLAYWRIGHT: One is light-skinned, one dark . . .

ANDRÉ: And both of them no doubt nose-pickers who speak the English language badly. I knew I shouldn't have asked.

PLAYWRIGHT: They live in a pondok in one of the local slums . . .

ANDRÉ *(Horror)*: Enough! No wonder London wasn't interested, dear boy. This world is ugly enough as it is for heaven's sake. People go to the theatre to be elevated above its squalor and filth, not to have it thrown in their faces. What's the name for these new plays? Kitchen-sink dramas?

PLAYWRIGHT: That's a few notches up from the world I'm writing about. There's no kitchen sink in my pondok. *(A laugh)* That is in fact what they dream about having. A genuine kitchen sink!

ANDRÉ: I give up! You're not taking me seriously.

Is it perversity that makes you devote the glorious energy of your young life, of whatever talent you've got, to crawling into stinking pondoks? Why? Explain to me.

PLAYWRIGHT: It's a world of untold stories. For any writer that's a gift from the gods.

ANDRÉ: Gift from the gods? What you've described to me is a nightmare.

PLAYWRIGHT: That's right. That's a good word to describe our slums—the South African nightmare. I know what I'm talking about, André. I saw a lot of those nightmares firsthand not long after we did *Oedipus* in Cape Town. Up in Johannesburg. Six months up there in the native commissioner's court. It was the only job I could find. I reckon that on an average day, between 8:30 in the morning and 4:30 in the afternoon, with a forty-five-minute lunch break, we sent a black person to jail every five minutes for not having the right stamp in their Dom Book. Should have seen it, André. It was pure Kafka. Simple innocent people being mangled by a legal process that the devil could have designed.

ANDRÉ: Yes, yes. I am sure it was all very sad and moving, but what has that to do with theatre?

PLAYWRIGHT: Everything . . . as far as my theatre is concerned.

ANDRÉ: Your theatre?

PLAYWRIGHT: Yes. You had yours; can't I have mine?

ANDRÉ: Oh by all means, dear boy—go ahead and have it! But just remember you're a white man, and try telling stories about your own people.

PLAYWRIGHT: If I find a good one I will.

ANDRÉ: What do you mean? You've already got it. It's staring you in the face.

(Pause. The Playwright does not know what he means.)

Your father for heaven's sake. Yes. You and your father. *(Bitter little laugh)* There'd be a good role for me in that one! And what's more you've already got your title: *A Man of No Importance.*

PLAYWRIGHT *(Angry and defensive)*: You know, André, that phrase you used . . . "your own people" . . . If you don't mind me saying so, that is exactly what is wrong with our theatre—with this whole damned country for that matter. Because as far as I'm concerned the people of the slums are also "my people." I can't pretend they don't exist. They're out there, and as much a part of my world as you, or my wife or the unborn child she is carrying or my dying father. I rub shoulders with them every day of my life—in my home when old Maria comes to clean up our mess; the beggars on the pavements. They're not invisible you know.

In some ways their world is even more real for me than the white one I live in.

(Pause.)

I would have stayed on in London and kept knocking on doors if it hadn't been for a front-page picture in the *Evening Standard.* It's pasted into my notebook. If you look very carefully you can count twelve bodies in it, though of course there were sixty-nine all told. Sharpeville. Just lying there on the ground, all of them face down in the dirt. They were running away when the police opened fire on a peaceful protest against the tyranny of those Dom Books. That did it! There's no way I could stay on in London after that.

ANDRÉ: And do you think your plays, or anybody else's for that matter, are going to make a difference?

PLAYWRIGHT: I don't know. But wasn't that the hope you had for your theatre . . . once upon a time? Wasn't it going to "wake up the Afrikaner and make him think"? Your words! Anyway, that's the only thing I can do. Like Marais, the blank page has become my home.

ANDRÉ: Well you'll be wasting your time, dear boy, as much as I wasted mine. If you are going to write, take my advice and learn how to write good drawing-room farces. That way you will make a lot of money and live happily ever afterwards. That is what I should have done. Wake up the Afrikaner and make him think? Did I really say that? What a fool! Look at them. It's worse now than when I started out thirty-five years ago. The Guardians of the volk have locked up this country and thrown away the key. If you think they are going to allow any changes you've got another guess coming.

PLAYWRIGHT: If that was true, if I really believed there was nothing we could do to change it . . . I don't know . . . maybe it would be time then for a suicide pact between us.

ANDRÉ (Sharply): Don't say that lightly!

PLAYWRIGHT (Also heating up): I'm not. Oh for God's sake, André, all I'm trying to say . . . oh never mind.

(A few seconds of strained silence between the two men. The Playwright breaks the moment.)

I'm sorry, André. All I wanted to do in coming back-stage was to tell you that your performance tonight was wonderful. (Looks at his watch) I must be on my way now.

ANDRÉ: You're going?

PLAYWRIGHT: Yep.

ANDRÉ *(A barely discernible edge of desperation)*: No. Not yet. What about a little nightcap, poephol. One for the road.

(The Playwright hesitates.)

Please. We haven't exhausted all our points of disagreement.

No . . . I won't take no for an answer. There are glasses at the back there—and a jug of water.

(André produces a half-jack of brandy. He pours them each a tot. A slightly awkward silence as they clink glasses and take their first sips. We sense that André wants to talk but doesn't know how to begin.)

PLAYWRIGHT: Don't your stage managers want to lock up? The bars close in half an hour.

ANDRÉ *(A parody of arrogant unconcern)*: That might well be, but that is no concern of mine. Don't you know who I am?

PLAYWRIGHT: Yes I do . . . and I don't think I will ever forget it.

ANDRÉ: Peter won't mind. He's a darling and he adores me. *(Trying to reestablish the warm intimacy of their relationship)* You didn't take offense did you?

PLAYWRIGHT: At what?

ANDRÉ: My little spasm of impatience with your "vision."

PLAYWRIGHT: Not at all.

ANDRÉ: It's just that you reminded me a little too much of myself when I was your age. He is the André you should have known. You two would have got on well together. Soul mates! All that's left of his vision now are a few sunbleached old posters peeling away on walls in small platteland towns where he wasted away his talent.

PLAYWRIGHT: No. Don't say that. Just five years ago we celebrated your thirty years in Theatre, and every night
audiences in the Labia Theatre gave you a standing ovation for a magnificent performance. Have you forgotten
that?

ANDRÉ: No. But I wish I had!
Do you know how and where I ended up after that
"celebratory production"?

PLAYWRIGHT: No.

ANDRÉ: Flat broke and dressed up like a performing monkey
in the lobby of a cheap bughouse bioscope in Joburg.
Yes! I was the manager of the Pigalle Cinema where
cheap Hollywood trash was getting bigger audiences in
a week than I had ever played to in a whole year. The
only qualification I had needed for that job was my
frayed, old, evening dress-suit and down-at-heel shiny
patent-leather black shoes. *(A helpless gesture)* It was the
only work I could find. I've been left behind by time—
relegated to the museum of Afrikaner cultural oddities.
You see, my acting style was "too old-fashioned," "too
over-the-top," my manner "too affected," as one critic
put it, for the new South African theatre, and I have a
sneaking feeling that you are that. Be honest with me,
would you want to cast me as one of your brothers in
that smelly pondok?

PLAYWRIGHT: Why not? You played Ample.

ANDRÉ: He was white and an Afrikaner . . . and I was young.

PLAYWRIGHT: The performance I saw tonight . . .

ANDRÉ: Stop. Don't be kind. Not tonight. Let us remember
our reunion as a moment of truth . . . and anyway there
is a sort of happy ending to my sad story you know. The
lobby of the Pigalle turned out to be a blessing in disguise because as things worked out it was actually a
rehearsal room for the performance you saw tonight.
I didn't know it at the time, but in being reduced to

standing there at the door, tearing ticket stubs in half and telling little snotneuses, who were feeling up their girlfriends in the back row, to take their feet off the seats and their hands off her tits, terrified that one of my admirers from the past would come in and see where the great André Huguenet had ended up, dying every day of humiliation and shame, I was in fact preparing for my farewell performance. *(Cuts short a gesture of protest from the Playwright)* Oh yes—that is what it is. What you saw tonight is the last one. But damned good casting, don't you think? I've never fitted a role so perfectly. André Huguenet as the Cardinal, a proud, conceited prince of the Church who is slowly stripped of all his disguises and forced to recognize and confess to what he really is. But the most extraordinary thing about the performance you saw is that for the first time ever I was doing something on the stage "for real." Instead of standing aside and watching my antics as Hamlet or Hassan, thinking all the time how clever an actor I was, and wasn't the audience lucky to have me up there, what I was doing this time was as real as my breathing or my heartbeat. And do you know what it was? Praying. Yes. You saw André Huguenet pray tonight. The last time I had done that was when I was growing up in Bloemfontein. The angelic Little Predikant was always kneeling at his bedside asking the Almighty to rain down his wrath on the bully boys who were tormenting the little Dopper Moffie. I thought of God as my personal bouncer. When I eventually realized he wasn't doing a good job I fired him and resorted to juvenile spite to right the many wrongs done against me. It was a very different story up there as the Cardinal. Down on my knees, scrubbing the floor of my cell, I truly scrubbed and I truly prayed. ". . . May he not slumber that keepeth thee. Behold He shall neither slumber nor sleep that keepeth Israel. The Lord is thy keeper, the Lord is thy protection upon thy right hand . . . In nomine Patris et Filii, et Spiritus Sancti. Amen."

Amazing isn't it, that in my thirty years of acting, that role alone has taught me something useful. It's true. Oedipus didn't teach me to curb my tongue or my temper. Lear didn't prepare me for the lobby of the Pigalle Cinema. Or Hamlet? Oh yes . . . I was also up there on the battlements of Elsinore trying to look beautiful and ask that big question, which I ended up thinking was just a literary conceit. I could go through the entire list of roles I have played and at the end what did they all add up to?—an aging old gay ham as full of arrogance and conceit as the pretentious young fool I was at your age.

God knows how I would have played the Cardinal, or had the wisdom to realize it was my last one, if it hadn't been for the Pigalle Cinema and the lesson it taught me. You hit the nail on the head my boy when you used the word "humility"! That is what you are left with when your pride, your vanity, your selfishness is slowly stripped away. And dear God how that hurts! You must understand, dear boy, those qualities weren't something I wore like a stage costume or that old evening dress-suit, to put on and take off as the occasion demanded. They had become my second nature, a skin of living flesh, the very surface of my being—and every torn ticket stub in my hand as I stood there in the lobby of the Pigalle was another piece of that skin torn away from my being. I was flayed alive in that lobby. But there again: blessings in disguise! When I left the Pigalle I was ready to go down on my knees and pray. I do it now in my hotel room. Do you pray?

PLAYWRIGHT: No. Like you I went through the motions in my childhood but it also meant nothing to me. What do you pray for, André?

ANDRÉ: Nothing very much. A little courage. That's all. I mean, damnit! If the Cardinal can be made brave enough to go out into the world and face his fellow men as the man he truly is, couldn't the same mercy be extended to me? I am also desperate to escape from my cell and stand in the light of day as my true self. Wear my curse—the Dopper Moffie—as a badge of honor and not one of disgrace.

(Pause.)

Oh dear me! I'm all emotional tonight . . . and it's all your fault.

(Pause. He looks intently at the young man.)

Brace yourself, darling, because now I'm going to embarrass you even more. I want to give you something. No . . . no . . . don't say anything. Just promise me you won't laugh.

PLAYWRIGHT: Promise.

ANDRÉ: And don't get your hopes up, either, because all you're going to get from me is a blessing. It's mine to give to you because I got it one night in Pretoria from no less a person than Eugène Marais. It is so appropriate! You see, our little tête-à-tête tonight is an almost perfect replay of that occasion between young Gerhardus Petrus Borstlap and Oom Eugène—hope-filled youth aflame with its vision talking to defeated and despairing age. He listened with such patience to my dream of an Afrikaans theatre, and before he left he gave it and me his blessing. That's what I'm giving you now: "Fan the flames of your purpose. Make it burn as big and bright as you can."

PLAYWRIGHT: Thank you, André.

41

ANDRÉ: It was late at night in the office of *Die Vaderland*—a newspaper in Pretoria. I had gone there to write a review about a bad performance. After writing my review, and with an eye to the great future that lay ahead of me, I decided I would practice Hamlet's famous soliloquy—I had a book of Shakespeare's plays in the drawer of my desk. I thought I already knew it by heart and was speaking it aloud, you know *(In his conversational voice, making no attempt at performance)*: "To be, or not to be— that is the question . . ." Et cetera, et cetera . . . Somewhere along the way I made a mistake and suddenly there was a voice out of the darkness correcting me. I knew who it was immediately of course—Oom Eugène!—it was a voice you never forgot. It was dark you see and I hadn't noticed him at his desk when I came in. In those last few years he had been reduced to writing silly stories for magazines so as to pay the rent, which he never did anyway because all his money went to his addiction. That is why he was in the office that night. His hypodermic syringe and all the other paraphernalia were on the desk in front of him. He got very embarrassed when he realized I had seen them, not that I didn't already know. Everybody knew what Oom Eugène was up to when he thought our backs were turned.

Trained as I already was as an actor, I took his prompt and carried on, until he corrected me again and then, a few lines further, yet again, after which he took over the soliloquy himself. He knew it by heart and he was word perfect.

(André shakes his head, speechless for a moment as the memory of Marais comes back to him.)

Sitting there spellbound at my desk, I was an audience for what must surely be one of the most remarkable deliveries that soliloquy has ever had! He wasn't an actor on a stage, puffed up with vanity and thinking of the review in the morning paper—he was talking from the heart. *(Looks at the Playwright and waits, as if expecting a response)* You don't get it, do you? Neither did I at the time. He was debating his suicide. It wasn't Hamlet asking, "To be, or not to be?" It was Eugène Marais; it was his question and he answered it five years later when he went for a walk in the Transvaal veld and never came back.

PLAYWRIGHT: What happened?

ANDRÉ: He shot himself.

PLAYWRIGHT: Why?

ANDRÉ: The calamity of too long a life. His creativity was exhausted and he knew it. Poor Eugène! He's been a lot in my thoughts lately.

I finally got my chance to play the Prince of Denmark, you know . . . Unfortunately I wasn't ready for it yet. I am now. You see, Marais was so right—"To be, or not to be" is not a literary conceit, it is a real question:

Is it nobler in the mind to suffer
The slings and arrows of outrageous fortune,
Or to take arms against a sea of troubles,
And by opposing end them?

(André is now committed to the full soliloquy.)

To die—to sleep—
No more; and by a sleep to say we end
The heartache, and the thousand natural shocks
That flesh is heir to, 'tis a consummation
Devoutly to be wish'd. To die—to sleep?
To sleep, perchance to dream. Ay, there's the rub;
For in that sleep of death what dreams may come
When we have shuffled off this mortal coil,

Must give us pause. There's the respect
That makes calamity of so long life;
For who would bear the whips and scorns of time,
Th'oppressor's wrong, the proud man's contumely,
The pangs of disprized love, the law's delay,
The insolence of office, and the spurns
That patient merit of th'unworthy takes,
When he himself might his quietus make
With a bare bodkin? Who would these fardels bear,
To grunt and sweat under a weary life,
But that the dread of something after death,
The undiscover'd country, from whose bourn
No traveler returns, puzzles the will,
And makes us rather bear those ills we have
Than fly to others that we know not of?
Thus conscience does make cowards of us all,
And thus the native hue of resolution
Is sicklied o'er with the pale cast of thought,
And enterprises of great pith and moment
With this regard their currents turn awry
And lose the name of action.

(The Playwright leaves the scene with André. He goes to his writing desk, where he sat writing at the beginning of the play. It is 1961. André remains seated in an old armchair sipping brandy—a lonely figure—until the end of the play.)

PLAYWRIGHT *(Speaking directly to the audience)*: And then this morning I spotted that little news item reporting his death in Bloemfontein. There was of course no mention of the circumstances. And that is as far as my story about him can go. As that broody Prince of Denmark himself says with his last breath: "The rest is silence."

There is a moment in *The Prisoner* when the Cardinal says to his Interrogator, "I am not, you know, beloved. I am not a likeable man." André said it onstage with a note of such quiet and unshakeable conviction you just knew he believed it was true of himself. He was wrong. But that's enough about André for tonight. I'm sure I'll be thinking about him again. My last entry of the day *(Reads from his notebook)*:

I will lie in bed tonight and as I have done so many nights, I will watch the shadow of a tree on our little stoep outside the open French doors. The lace curtains will breathe gently, with a soft wind, and the shadow itself will move, clotting into blackness on the cool stone stoep or breaking apart into the agitated contours of leaves; and, as has happened on so many nights now, I will fall asleep in the unimportant labyrinth of a dialogue that I follow through as if learnt by rote. First my mind consciously analyzes the phenomenon of a shadow, the fall of light, etc., and it assures me that a shadow is nothing, its reality as insubstantial as the characters I create on paper or that André gave life to on the stage. Then with my eyes, with all the senses of my living mortal body, I look at "it"— "it"—and savor the beauty of its being. Yet it is nothing. My mind has told me so and proved it. And then my wonder increases, encompassing now not only the beauty of the shadow itself but the duplicity, the paradox that runs so richly through all this life. And then sleep.

(He exits, leaving André alone onstage.)

END OF PLAY

Glossary

AFRIKAANS	The language derived from the Dutch first settlers of the Cape
APPLOUS: DIE KRONIEKE VAN 'N TONEELSPELER	*Applause: The Chronicle of an Actor*
BOERESEUN	Farmer's son
BRAAIVLEIS	Barbeque
COLOREDS	Defined in South Africa as anyone of mixed racial descent
DOM BOOK	Passbook, ID book for black people under apartheid
DOPPER	Strict religious sect of the Dutch Reform Church
DOPPER MOFFIE	A "queer" in the Dopper community
DRC	Dutch Reform Church

GLOSSARY

EERLIKHEID EN CHRISTELIKHEID	Honor and religion—Dutch Reform Church
GUARDIANS OF THE VOLK	Protectors of the people
HALF-AAN-DIE-SLAAP DOMKOPPE	Half-asleep idiots
HOU JOU FOCKIN BEK! LUIS GAT!	"Shut the fuck up! Lazy ass!"
KAROO	A vast semi-desert region in the heart of South Africa; "karoo" is a Khoi word meaning "place of little water"; few plants grow on the dry mountains, but farms thrive in the valleys and lowlands
OOM	Uncle
OPREGTE	Genuine
POEPHOL	Asshole (can be an affectionate term)
PONDOK	Shanty
PREDIKANT	Preacher
REPUBLIEK	Republic
SNOT EN TRANE	Snot and tears
SNOTNEUS	Snot nose
STAATS	States
STOEP	Porch
TACKIES	Tennis shoes
VELD	Countryside

Glossary

VERKRAMPTE	Narrow-minded
VERVLOEKTE	Cursed
VOLK	People

$\mathcal{A}fterword$

By Marianne McDonald

IN ADDITION to tracing his own personal journey, most of Athol Fugard's plays reflect moments in the history of South Africa. He has said that the end of apartheid freed him from the burden of guilt he carried as a white man and allowed him to write plays that were more overtly autobiographical, or even about Hildegard of Bingen (*The Abbess*, 2000), plays that might have been considered an indulgence in the old South Africa. *Exits and Entrances* is the most recent of the autobiographical plays in which Fugard details his formative experience with an important mentor.

The opening scene takes place in the year 1961, a momentous year for South Africa, for theatre and, indeed, for Fugard himself. It was the year South Africa withdrew from the British Commonwealth and declared itself an independent republic. It was just one year after the infamous Sharpeville massacre, when sixty-nine blacks were shot dead for protesting the white supremacist policy of apartheid. It was also the year the famous Afrikaner actor and director André Huguenet died. And for Fugard, it was the year his father died; the year his wife, Sheila, gave birth to their daughter, Lisa; and the year his play *Blood Knot*, in which he first found his own voice, reached the stage and became his first commercial success, at home and abroad.

Exits and Entrances is based on two meetings (in 1956 and 1961) between a character called the Playwright—Fugard himself, though never named as such—and André Huguenet. In the 1956 meeting, André is fifty-one and the Playwright is twenty-four. In 1961, André, fifty-six, is about to end his life, whereas the Playwright, at twenty-nine, is flush with impending fatherhood and critical acclaim.

The play opens on the night the new republic was born, with the Playwright in his Port Elizabeth apartment reading about André's death and writing in his notebook. (Fugard's notebooks have been his constant companions for a number of years. He uses them to comment on his life, the life of South Africa, and his work process.)

As the Playwright reminisces about Huguenet, the play flashes back to 1956 and a dressing room in Cape Town's Labia Theatre. The Playwright, who is just embarking on his writing career, is acting in a production of *Oedipus Rex* with André, who has given him his first acting job as the Shepherd. He is also acting as André's dresser, factotum, and general dogsbody, fixing honey tea, prompting him in his lines and bolstering André's ego, while André laces their conversation with acerbic, sometimes sarcastic, wit. The two men enjoy an obvious camaraderie; though clearly in charge, André is genuinely supportive of the younger man, and the Playwright is in awe of André's genius.

André asks the Playwright about his plans, gently points out the difficulties of becoming a playwright, and speaks of his own dreams as a boy and young man. Raised in a conventional Afrikaner household that shared the motto of his school, "Eerlikheid en Christelikheid" ("honor and religion"; in this case the Dutch Reform Church), he was nicknamed "Dopper Moffie" (see Glossary) by "the big bully boys . . . because he didn't play rugby with them."

Huguenet says he realized that art was his calling one night in 1916 when he risked damnation—his family was grooming him for the church—by sneaking out of the house to see the legendary Russian ballet dancer Anna Pavlova: "The devil had sent her because of all the sinning that was going on in Bloemfontein, which, of course, meant that I just had to see her for myself." Once he saw her dance her signature solo, "The Dying Swan," he was lost to his family, and won over to a life in theatre, forever. He realized that her beauty and her consummate art came from her dreams:

> Somewhere along the line she had to believe she was the most beautiful, the most graceful of all the creatures in the world, and to believe that with every fiber of her being and, having dreamt that, she also had to feel the first touch of death and try, hopelessly, to escape it, discover that her magnificent wings could no longer lift her off the ground, feel that touch turn into a cruel, unrelenting hold on her whole life . . .

One might call this an existentialist manifesto, and Camus's definition of life through death, besides describing the life of Huguenet himself, can be seen in most of Fugard's writing.

The second encounter between the two men takes place in another dressing room, this time at the Port Elizabeth Opera House. By now, André's star is falling, but the Playwright's is rising. Huguenet has introduced European classics to the South Africa stage, while the Playwright has found his vocation in telling South African stories.

This scene segues back to the Playwright's apartment. He closes his notebook and exits, leaving André, now a figure of memory, seated alone and lonely in an armchair, sipping brandy. Parallels abound: the birth of a country, a new life, and a new play that signals a new playwright. At the same time, two "fathers"—one genetic and one spiritual—die. "Exits and entrances," indeed.

Harold Athol Lanigan Fugard was born on June 11, 1932, in Middelburg, Great Karoo, Cape Province, South Africa. His mother was of Afrikaner background; his father was a pianist and an alcoholic who was crippled in an accident and died when Fugard was twenty-nine.

In a *New Yorker* profile by Mel Gussow (December 20, 1982), Fugard attributed his passionate sense of justice to his mother:

> Like Piet Bezuidenhout in *A Lesson from Aloes* [Fugard, 1981], she had this set of ideas and human values that put her in radical opposition to the system [apartheid] . . . She never got involved in politics, but as early as I can remember she had an understanding of the injustice. I think that all the faith I have in life and in people . . . comes to me from my mother.

Actor and director André Huguenet, celebrated as the "Olivier of South Africa," was born Gerhardus Petrus Borstlap in 1906 in Bloemfontein and died in 1961. At age twenty, he joined Paul de Groot's theatre company, but his parents wanted him to become a minister, so he began studying for a bachelor's degree at the University College of the Orange Free State. However, he soon left college and returned to acting.

In 1931, he founded his own acting company in the Cape, and changed his name to André Huguenet. (In Afrikaans, "borstlap" suggests "wet dishrag," so the name change marked his entrance into the world of South African theatre with an appropriate flourish.) The company performed new works and classics in Afrikaans—Huguenet was most attracted to the works of Shakespeare, Ibsen and the ancient Greeks—but failed to meet with financial success. He eventually disbanded his company and, in 1937, went to London, where he worked with the British Drama League and toured Europe and Russia. He then returned to South Africa, where he founded a series of companies; toured America, in 1941; and joined the National Theatre Organisation of South Africa. Among his greatest roles was Hamlet, for which he was awarded the Queen's Coronation Medal in 1947. He also was acclaimed for the title role in *Hassan*, a tragic love story by the British diplomat and orientalist James Elroy Flecker; André playfully gives a taste of his performance in that play to the young Playwright in *Exits and Entrances*. In 1950, he was invited to perform that role in London and became the first South African actor ever invited to England to play a specific role. He was also invited to the Netherlands to play the leading role in the medieval play *Jedermann* (*Everyman*), a religious play that warns its audience to make peace with God or suffer the consequences when death arrives unannounced. Among his other major roles were the hypochondriac from Molière's *Le Malade Imaginaire* and Oedipus from Sophocles' *Oedipus the King*, which he performed in Afrikaans in South Africa (he later played Oedipus in English as well); and Macbeth. He also performed in films.

By 1959, his career began to decline, but he still played the King in Shakespeare's *King Lear* in 1960. His final performances, as the Cardinal in *The Prisoner*, by the late Irish playwright and screenwriter Bridget Boland, took place in 1961 at the Port Elizabeth Opera House. Based on the imprisonment of the Hungarian Cardinal Josef Mindszenty, the play concerns a cardinal, imprisoned as a political agitator by an oppressive regime in an unnamed middle

European country, who is forced by an interrogator to face his own hypocrisy and pride. For Huguenet, the play gave voice to his own despair and feelings of entrapment. About a month after the play ended, he died at his sister's house in Bloemfontein. Suicide? Perhaps his final role was his own choice.

Exits and Entrances quotes and reenacts passages from many of Huguenet's most famous roles. These scenes are particularly moving because they describe him at each point in his life. His roles were delivered with blood and guts, and, at one point, when he plays the blinded Oedipus, he says, "I've come to love the taste of that stage blood dripping from my face."

The Playwright brings to life the genius of André's impeccable timing in his chilling and graphic description of André's agonized cry when, as Oedipus, he realizes that he has murdered his father and married and mated with his mother, and is both father and brother to his own children:

> André, as Oedipus, standing at the top of the steps in front of the doors of his Theban palace, became very still, and we ordinary mortals held our breaths and waited. In those terribly silent seconds it seemed as if the whole world was waiting, and at the point when you thought you could no longer endure it and would have to scream, at that precise moment, not a second too soon or too late, André opened his mouth and out of it came the most awful cry that any member of that audience had ever heard. It sounded as if he had somehow reached down deep into himself and was dragging his genitals up through his body and throat and hanging them out of his mouth for all of us to spit on and curse.

In scenes like these, Fugard makes clear that André's acting was his own lifeblood and that his roles were his life.

André says he was finally humbled, as the Cardinal was, and that he has learned how to pray. He is now desperate to stand in the light of day as his true self, to "wear my curse— the 'Dopper Moffie'—as a badge of honor and not one of disgrace." This confession is the climax of André's own despair, the hope he knows will never be realized in his country at this time. It could have been in post-apartheid South Africa, particularly after 1994 with its free election and a new constitution.

PLAYWRIGHT: This is where the play starts to get scary.
You know what little Jennifer—your Antigone—said to me this afternoon? "Why doesn't he stop and listen to the prophet and his wife. That way we could have a happy ending tonight."
ANDRÉ *(An exultant, almost brutal laugh)*: "Stop and listen"? He can't! He is Oedipus!
PLAYWRIGHT: And so are you.
ANDRÉ: What do you mean?
PLAYWRIGHT: Just what you said earlier. You are like him in so many ways.
ANDRÉ: Those being . . . my temper?
PLAYWRIGHT: That's one for sure. We're all terrified of you.
ANDRÉ: But what else?

(The young Playwright is reluctant to say more.)

Come on! Speak up, boy.
PLAYWRIGHT: There! The way you said that.
ANDRÉ: I see. Arrogance.
PLAYWRIGHT: You could call it that.

But arrogance, or *hubris*, as the Greeks called it, did not blind Huguenet as it did Oedipus. He introduced theatre of quality to people who were not ready for it, and he knew they were not ready for it. No one is ever ready for the revolutions that have led to major cultural changes. André was one of the sacrifices along the way, but it did not deter him. Like Oedipus, he carried on until he could carry on no longer. The small audiences finally bankrupted him. His country awarded him high honors—but ultimately rejected him. In many ways, André's story parallels Fugard's: he too had to find his greatest success outside his own country because he violated the boundaries of the acceptable in South Africa. Fugard was the Socratic critic of his country, the Euripides of his time, and when an author holds "the mirror up to nature ... and the very age and body of the time"—Hamlet's definition of the purpose of theatre—he does so at his peril. As T. S. Eliot wrote in "Burnt Norton," "Human kind / Cannot bear very much reality." Neither could Huguenet. As Oedipus, he admits his crimes:

> I alone am polluted:
> I am the only man who must bear this suffering.

Even this confession, though, betrays his godlike arrogance.

When the Playwright reminisces about their second meeting, André is playing his final role, the Cardinal. Again, André delivers lines that capture his situation—in this case, a speech that shows the Cardinal trying to stave off despair and hang on to his sanity. Just as the Cardinal assumed masks to achieve his success, André confesses his own sins to the Playwright through the mask of the Cardinal:

> Let them see me in the weakness of the flesh and
> the meanness of the spirit. That will be degradation,

that will be shame enough to burn the past and come through the flames, free.

Like Oedipus, the Cardinal suffers from pride; but while Oedipus never fully learns the lessons of humility, even when he is reduced to begging in *Oedipus at Colonus*, the Cardinal does. André tells the Playwright that he, too, was forced to learn humility when he was reduced to working as a lowly movie theatre usher and ticket-taker to survive. He dreaded seeing someone from his past; he wanted no witnesses to his fall. Like the Cardinal, he finally learned what it meant to be humble.

When the Playwright tells André that he has written a play (*Blood Knot*) about the rivalry between two colored brothers, one dark and one light-skinned, living in a pondok ("shanty"), André asks, "Kitchen-sink dramas?" The Playwright answers, "That's a few notches up from the world I'm writing about. There's no kitchen sink in my pondok." André reveals his own limitations as he speaks disparagingly of this type of drama and cynically encourages the younger man to write drawing-room comedies if he wants to be a success. He adds, "But just remember you're a white man, and try telling stories about your own people." The Playwright answers, "If I find a good one I will." As history and international recognition have proven, he did. Fugard finally attained what Huguenet had dreamed of.

The two men discuss their ideals, the Playwright reminding André that he once intended to "wake up the Afrikaner and make him think." The Playwright is trying to do the same, but André has given up hope:

> The Guardians of the volk have locked up this country and thrown away the key. If you think they are going to allow any changes you've got another guess coming.

The Playwright, however, has not given up hope. He lives to see the end of apartheid. In a possible reference to suicide, André announces that *The Prisoner* will be his last performance. Still, he continues an affectionate conversation, calling the Playwright "poephol" (literally "asshole," but untranslatable since the term in Afrikaans lacks the insulting connotation it has in English).

André says he was finally humbled, as the Cardinal was, and he has learned how to pray. He is now desperate to escape from his cell, he says, and to stand in the light of day as his true self, to "wear my curse—the Dopper Moffie—as a badge of honor and not one of disgrace."

In addition to speaking of the Playwright's apprenticeship and articulating Huguenet's philosophy of drama and his coming to terms with death, the play refers at length to another important figure in South African cultural history—Eugène Marais (1871–1936), the famous naturalist and poet who was the subject of Fugard's screenplay *The Guest* (1977). Marais, a longtime morphine addict, shot himself—a possible link with Huguenet. André passes his blessing on to the Playwright just as Marais had once blessed him: the blessing of one creator, who understands existential despair, to another.

André recalls a decisive encounter with Marais in his youth. They read the "to be or not to be" soliloquy together. Both Marais and Huguenet made this passage, which debates the choice of living or dying, their own. One was a drug addict, and the other a homosexual; both were living on the margins of their society, "strangers" or "outsiders" in the sense that Camus used the term, yet both made vital contributions to the cultural life of South Africa and the world. We know Marais's all-too-final decision, which was also very possibly Huguenet's, but Fugard voted for life. As he earlier paid tribute to Marais in *The Guest*, now he has immortalized Huguenet, this complex figure who brought great theatre in the form of the classics to South Africa. Huguenet not only brought the classics—he lived them. His life was a Greek tragedy in every sense of the word, complete with the same awesome tragic majesty.

In 1951 Fugard began attending the University of Cape Town, where he majored in philosophy, sociology, anthropology and French. However, he left in his third year, before his final examinations, to hitchhike up Africa, and ended up sailing around the world on a tramp steamer, the S. S. *Graigaur*. After returning to Port Elizabeth, he wrote freelance articles for the *Evening Post* and later worked as a news reporter for the South African Broadcasting Corporation. In 1956, he married writer Sheila Meiring.

Fugard wrote and appeared in his first plays in 1956, but later destroyed those early manuscripts. It was during this period that he met and worked with André Huguenet. In 1958, he left a job with the native commissioner's court in Johannesburg to become a stage manager for the National Theatre Organisation. The same year, his play *No-Good Friday* was workshopped in Sophiatown, a suburb of Johannesburg.

In 1959, the Fugards went to England, where they worked in and around the theatre scene in London and Western Europe. In 1961, provoked by the Sharpeville massacre, they returned to Port Elizabeth. In 1967, in an apparent attempt to coerce Fugard into leaving the country, the government took away his passport. Without it, Fugard could leave the country, but could not return. But he refused to conform, toughing it out in spite of raids and hardship, and continued writing plays that chronicled the emergence of official apartheid, and then the transition from apartheid to the first free election in 1994. In 1971, he regained his passport. He now divides his time between homes in South Africa and Southern California.

He has just completed his thirty-sixth play. Many of these have been filmed, with Fugard acting in several. He has also acted in other films, including *Meetings with Remarkable Men* (1979), *Gandhi* (1982) and *The Killing Fields* (1984). His novel *Tsotsi* (2005) won an Academy Award for Best Foreign Film, among other awards, and his work has garnered many prizes both in South Africa and abroad. He has received more than twenty honorary degrees from universities throughout the world. He has also been elected a fellow of the British Royal Society of Literature (1986) and a member of the American Academy of Arts and Letters (1988).

There are many ways to classify Fugard's plays, either by their geographical setting or, more broadly, as family plays, problem plays, apartheid plays or mythical plays. Obviously many of these categories overlap. Fugard, however, has shaped the autobiographical play to make it truly his own. Other playwrights—Eugene O'Neill and Arthur Miller, for example—have taken elements from their lives and woven them into their drama, but few have done so as explicitly and frequently as Fugard has.

Before *Blood Knot*, a metaphorical depiction of the racial tensions in South Africa and also a warning to defenders of apartheid, Fugard's work showed traces of Tennessee Williams and Eugene O'Neill, two major early influences. With that play and the advent of the new South Africa, Fugard's work has progressed steadily toward a more personal idiom. This is especially true of the plays which take place in Nieu Bethesda, located in the beautiful semi-desert (Karoo) area and set in a valley surrounded by mountains, where Fugard was born and has had a home since 1972. Biographical elements have been present in all his plays— from inspiring *Blood Knot*, which he says was based on his relationship with his brother (although neither was colored), to a host of personal connections and associations in *Sorrows and Rejoicings* (2001), and finally to explicit autobiography in the most recent plays. The earlier Township plays, or those set in Port Elizabeth or imaginary places, were less personal.

Also, autobiographical material in the earlier works was often covert—for example, he has called himself "Miss Helen in drag," referring to the rebellious artist Helen Martins in *The Road to Mecca* (1984)—but it has become overt in the most recent works, as in the Playwright's role in *Exits and Entrances*.

Exits and Entrances is the third in the series of autobiographical plays that trace Fugard's development as a writer, following *"Master Harold"* . . . *and the boys* (1982) and *The Captain's Tiger* (1998). The author figure is also present in *Valley Song* (1995), but this character could just as well have been a businessman for all that we learn about his craft. Now, *Visions and Dreams* (2007), along with the other plays Fugard is currently working on, add a new installment.

"Master Harold" . . . *and the boys*, written when Fugard was fifty, is more objective than the autobiographical plays that followed. Set in Port Elizabeth at the St. George's Park Tea Room, the play centers around the bullying that "Hally" (representing Fugard as a white boy of seventeen) inflicts on two mature black men, Sam Semela and Willie Malopo, who work for his parents. Fugard modeled both characters on real men. In the play, Sam is Hally's surrogate father just as Huguenet later becomes Fugard's inspirational father. In *"Master Harold,"* Fugard takes the rules of apartheid to an extreme and has Hally bully "the boys" not only because this is the way he was raised, but also because their relationship is his only position of power, given the poverty of the family and his duties taking care of both of his parents.

Hally needs to learn the lessons articulated in the dance metaphor used in the play, just as South Africa eventually had to learn those same lessons. Sam tells him that, on the dance floor,

> There are no collisions out there, Hally . . . To be one
> of those finalists on that dance floor is like . . . like

being in a dream about a world in which accidents don't happen . . . And it's beautiful because that is what we want life to be like.

In *The Captain's Tiger*, written fifteen years later, Fugard, at sixty-five, looks back on himself at age twenty-one, when he sailed around the world as a "tiger," or personal servant to the ship's captain. The plot focuses on two parallel stories. One concerns Donkeyman, a Swahili sailor who befriends him and becomes, like Sam, a surrogate father. In the other, Fugard describes his own writing development by holding imaginary conversations with his mother, who functions as his muse. He gradually learns to be honest with his writing, and, at the end of the play, he destroys the novel he had been writing about her because he realizes that he has not been telling the truth, but rather adopting the imitative conceits of a fledgling writer.

Valley Song is autobiographical to the extent that the play is set at a time when Fugard was buying a house, which he still owns in Nieu Bethesda, and the character who represents him, the Author, is in his sixties, the same age as the real author. However, the Author is only tangential to the main storyline, which concerns a young colored girl who wants to leave her home and make her career in the city against the wishes of her grandfather. Her grandfather eventually realizes he must allow his granddaughter her freedom, just as the new South Africa finally enfranchised the black and colored people who had been without a vote under apartheid.

Valley Song is also the first of Fugard's plays in which he, as the Author, speaks to the audience. As early as *Sizwe Bansi Is Dead* (1972), *The Island* (1973) and *Statements After an Arrest Under the Immorality Act* (1974), characters in Fugard's plays address the audience, but his recent plays have a particular intensity, as if he has finally found his own voice after a lifetime of resisting so many people's attempts to silence him.

Though other plays draw on autobiographical elements, they do so less explicitly and sometimes metaphorically. For example, in *Sorrows and Rejoicings*, which is also set in Nieu Bethesda, Fugard identified with elements of the main character, Dawid, a writer who leaves South Africa during the apartheid years, becomes an alcoholic and finally returns to Nieu Bethesda to die of cancer. Fugard has said that he has often felt like an exile whenever he has had to spend extended periods outside South Africa because of his work, either directing his plays or acting in them. Nevertheless, he never left permanently, even during the years when his passport was taken from him, nor has he taken the citizenship of any other country. In addition, both he and Dawid suffered from alcoholism, although Fugard became sober in 1980. Fugard wrote about his personal journey and escape from alcoholism in the 1987 parable play, *A Place with the Pigs*, about a Russian deserter who hides in a pigsty but finally leaves his hideout and accepts the consequences of his actions.

In 2007, Fugard finished *Visions* and *Dreams*, two short plays. *Visions* was inspired by the "outsider" art of Nukain Mabusa, and tells a touching story of a grandfather near death, and a grandson taking over his creative role. The other play, *Dreams*, was inspired by the Swanker contest (begun under apartheid), a weekly competition in which working men fulfill their dreams by dressing up and assuming roles in which they aspire in life (businessmen, other men of means). Both plays show people being creative in ways that make life worth living, and also offer an example of Fugard's generous humor.

In 2008, Fugard attended rehearsals for *Victory* in Los Angeles (The Fountain Theatre), following successful performances in both South Africa and the Edinburgh Festival. The play is set in the Karoo, as is *Valley Song* (1995), but rather than a young girl aspiring to be an artist, *Victory* (2007) shows a young girl facing the problems of drug, crime and no opportunity, which is all too often the reality now in the new South Africa.

In 2004, Fugard attended several rehearsals of the premiere production of *Exits and Entrances* in Los Angeles, where he recounted anecdotes about Huguenet to help the actors understand the character of André. At one performance of *Oedipus Rex*, Fugard recalled, Huguenet was about to make his entrance after he had blinded himself and his face was streaming with stage blood. The two little girls playing Oedipus' daughter-sisters laughed at him, and it was obvious that they were about to ruin the performance by not weeping as they should when they went onstage. Huguenet turned to them in a fury and hissed, "If you don't cry when we get out there, I'll stick pins in you!" He would do anything, even threaten young actresses, to get a good performance.

During the *Exits* rehearsals, Fugard also decided to add material about his father to intensify the parallels between the failures of the two father figures in his life. At the same time, Fugard pointed out the great debt he owed his father for teaching him to love storytelling and music.

The Playwright spends much of the play listening to André and drawing on his ideas to shape his own vision of theatre, besides attempting to learn from the master actor what moves an audience. During the rehearsals, Fugard made the suggestion that William Dennis Hurley, the young actor playing the Playwright, listen even more intently so that the audience, too, would hang on to André's every word.

In this production, the metaphor of André's journey toward the truth of his life was reproduced by costume choices. As Oedipus, André wears an elaborate costume; as Hassan, he wears simply a dressing gown and a dressing-room towel wrapped about his head as a turban; as the Cardinal, he wears a tattered robe . . . and for the Hamlet soliloquy, delivered with simple truthfulness, he is stripped to just his underwear. André travels from an Oedipus searching for truth to a man who discovers it just before he dies. The audience sees him confess it to his one confidante, the Playwright. At the same time the Playwright journeys from conceited self-assurance, to self-doubt, to a tentative recognition of the writer that he is.

An early version of this play was simply about Huguenet and Marais, and was called *André and Eugène*, but Fugard eventually rewrote it to include the Playwright. This version was at first called *Entrances and Exits*, but the reversal *Exits and Entrances* conveys hope, including hope for the future of the Playwright's type of theatre, as well as for a whole new future for South Africa itself. André's final exit from life initiates the young man's entrance into his career as a full-fledged playwright.

Although Fugard's most recent plays deal with death and disillusionment, they also appreciate their protagonists' dreams. Fugard's telling of Huguenet's story is another instance of his giving a voice to those who have been silenced, for, although Huguenet wrote an autobiography, *Applause: The Chronicle of an Actor*, it is *Exits and Entrances* that lays bare the famous actor's soul.

Fugard's recent plays have taken the same path of truth and simplicity that Huguenet finally traveled. With this work, Fugard's superb command of his craft as a dramatist has created a sympathetic and understanding monument to Huguenet, an outstanding Afrikaner who shaped South African theatre and was its most outstanding actor. He proved that Afrikaans was a language that could convey any classic, but, although he won many awards, he never achieved either the artistic recognition or the financial success of which he dreamed.

Huguenet kindled Fugard's creative fire as powerfully as Pavlova ignited Huguenet's in 1916. In *Exits and Entrances*,

Fugard has created a tribute that will make Huguenet's story and accomplishments known throughout the world.

Other fires find their way into the works of these two men who, each in their own way, have captured the history of their country in masterpieces for the rest of the world to see. Great artists will always provide commentary on the world's horrors and try to light the way to change by the intensity of their passions and the torch of their conscience.

MARIANNE MCDONALD is Professor of Theatre and Classics in the Department of Theatre at the University of California, San Diego; a member of the Royal Irish Academy; and a recipient of many national and international awards. With 250 publications, her published books include: *Euripides in Cinema: The Heart Made Visible* (Centrum Press, 1983), *Ancient Sun, Modern Light: Greek Drama on the Modern Stage* (Columbia University Press, 1992); *Sing Sorrow: Classics, History and Heroines in Opera* (Greenwood, 2001) and *The Living Art of Greek Tragedy* (Indiana University Press, 2003). With J. Michael Walton, works include: *Amid Our Troubles: Irish Versions of Greek Tragedies* (Methuen, 2002) and *The Cambridge Companion to Greek and Roman Theatre* (2007). Unpublished works include: *Space, Time and Silence: The Craft of Athol Fugard*. Her performed translations include: Sophocles' *Antigone,* directed by Athol Fugard in Ireland (1999); Euripides' *Children of Heracles* (2003); Sophocles' *Oedipus Tyrannus* and *Oedipus at Colonus* (2003-2004); Euripides' *Hecuba* (2005); Sophocles' *Ajax* (2006); Euripides' *Iphigenia at Aulis* and *Bacchae* (2006) and Aeschylus' *Oresteia* (2007). Other translations/adaptations and original plays include: *The Trojan Women* (2000); *Medea, Queen of Colchester* (2003), *The Ally Way* (2004); *. . . and then he met a woodcutter* (San Diego Critics Circle's Best Play of 2005); *Medea: The Beginning,* performed with Athol Fugard's *Jason: The End* (2006) and *The Last Class* (2007). http://www.mmcdonald.info

South African–born playwright, actor and director ATHOL
FUGARD is one of the world's leading theatre artists. His
major works for the stage include: *Blood Knot* (1961);
Boesman and Lena (1969); *Statements After an Arrest Under the
Immorality Act* (1972); *Sizwe Bansi Is Dead* (1972); *The Island*
(1973); *A Lesson from Aloes* (1978); *"Master Harold"* . . . *and the
boys* (1982); *The Road to Mecca* (1984); *A Place with the Pigs:
A Personal Parable* (1987); *My Children! My Africa!* (1989);
Valley Song (1995); The *Captain's Tiger: A Memoir for the Stage*
(1997); *Sorrows and Rejoicings* (2001); *Exits and Entrances*
(2004); *Booitjie and the Oubaas* (2006); *Victory* (2007).
Awaiting Production: *The Abbess* (2000); *Visions* and *Dreams*
(two one-act plays, 2007).